a fix of ink

poems by

Cecilia Martinez-Gil

Finishing Line Press
Georgetown, Kentucky

a fix of ink

In Loving Memory of Terry Plumeri,
I'll see you "Across a River's Dream" my friend.

ACKNOWLEDGMENTS

"Moisten Harmonies" (1) is featured on a forthcoming album by musician
Alphonso Johnson.
"And the Letter Goes with the Sayings" (9). Ensemble of aphorisms from
Dictionary of Proverbs. Delfín Carbonell Basset, ed. Barron's. New York, 1998.
"Hiatus" (15). Quote by Jorge Luis Borges, Twenty-Four Conversations with
Borges: Interviews by Roberto Alifano 1981-1983.
"Whence Cometh Evil, Thy Sonnet I Shall Sing" (19). Ensemble of William
Shakespeare's Famous Phrases. goodreads. 2010. Web.
"Women of Newfalngleness" (43) alludes to "Women Who Run with Wolves," a
book by Clarisa Pinkola Estés.
"Suspension of Disbelief"(65). Reference to a quote by Christopher Priest, author
of *The Prestige*.

Publisher: Leah Maines

Editor: Christen Kincaid

Cover Art: Siolo Thompson

Author Photo: Oksana Godoy

Cover Design: Carolina Rivero, Siolo Thompson, and Isabel Baez Gil

Printed in the USA on acid-free paper.
Order online: www.finishinglinepress.com
            also available on amazon.com

Author inquiries and mail orders:
Finishing Line Press
P. O. Box 1626
Georgetown, Kentucky 40324
U. S. A.

Table of Contents

a Facebook Post as Preface

Moisten Harmony 1

in situ...2

Morpheus' Dream..3

Of Frogs and Angeles..4

writing outside the margins 5

bite the bullet...6

I lay bare..7

Transtrommer's Transmutations 8

And the Letter Goes with the Sayings 9

Thru Writing, Writing Truth...11

Residuals of Seduction..12

What Stays 13

Surviving Scales 14

Hiatus 15

Cryptic Blues...16

The Cyber Snatcher 17

From Whence Cometh Evil, Thy Sonnet I Shall Sing...................19

Leaning on a Shadow of Grey Hues 20

Typewriting 23

Inside the Inkwell 24

A Fix of Ink 26

Catharsis 28

waning gibbous language 30

Day 22: Waxing Crescent 31

Quills of a rare bird 33

Vi⊛gil in Dazetown...35

Capturing fall-nesses...37

Graffiti Sacrifice 38

(a)void..41

Tattoo 42

Women of Newfangleness..43

Trojan Horse 44

Abecedarian 46

Mentorship 48

Students and Professors 49

The Purloined Papers..52

Azar 54

Indigo Blur 55

Workshopping: indigo 57
Prewriting Exercise: fountain of ink 59
Dreamt 60
Draft: drink from my ink 61
Suspension of Disbelief 65
Vampires' Appeal to Dusk 66
Blogger in Bowtie 68
Epilogue 70
the word after 73

Hay que estar aéreo—en la cima de lo inesperado—para que, lo que adviene y en su celeridad demuda, mueva la túnica del estremecimiento y reciba la delicada excitación de la fugacidad requerida por lo eterno

One must remain aerial—at the summit of the unexpected—so, what is to come and in its haste is to alter us, move rather the tunic of thrill to receive the delicate enthrallment of the fugacity required by the eternal

Luis Eduardo Gil Salguero
Escritos, 1934-39
Trans. Cecilia Martinez-Gil

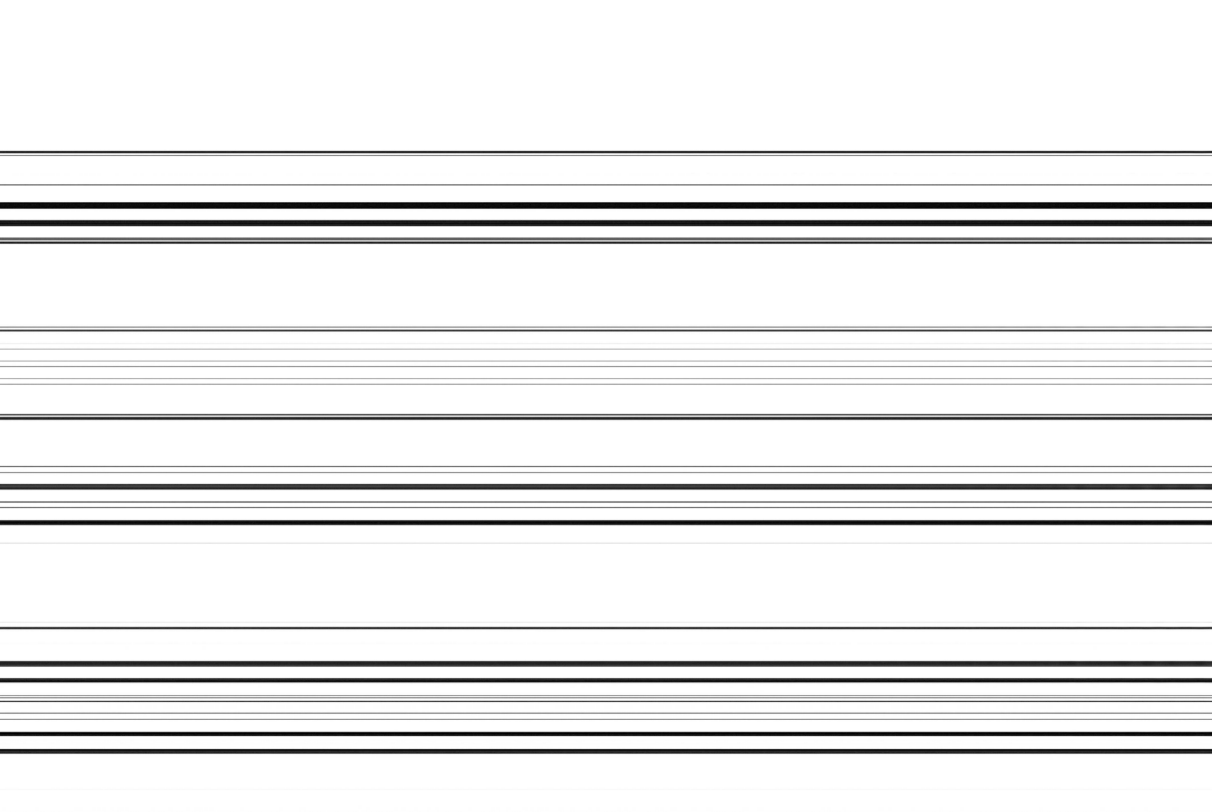

A, United States ·

day, I received the best
ng Line Press has chosen
and will be in print this
cond half of the journey
(that I don't trust bing
tinta." This collection of
three years of relentless
proofreading, it will be
st not use euphemisms
r, yeah, I have worked
n of my poems for this
ink.

a text is a space on the
creative realms where
and dreams, and the
ver, record and heal.
urvey of the history of
n, from the paintings
es to the language now
nication, on computer

studied with poet and
at LMU pursuing my
riting (class of 2012).
am Space" was based
gendered a chapbook
of ink bears now an
! working under the
fessor Gail Wronsky
enthal both, directors
or my Creative Master

Thesis, served many of the poe
to undergo their very first revis
many of the suggestions from
Thus, thank you Josie Colm
Templin, Donald Dilliplane, H
Lane, Stephanie Revy... In fact,
to when I read randomly, to
there, and meeting shamanistic
creation and creativity...Santiag
Scarlet Rivera, Eduardo Del Si
Maca, Carlos Daniel Lastra, Or
Clifford Bernier, David Miller, L
Hastings, Siolo Thompson, Reb
Terry Plumeri, Honor Chan..an
my work(s): Mario Rene Padilla

To make of this book even a
one of the poems of this colle
record by renown jazz music
maestro Alphonso Johnson, wh
year. The poem "Moisten Har
me accompanied by an origin
played by Gary Fukushima, and
as spoken word by superb musi
new sista. This poem speaks ab
birth it. Naturally, in this po
Ramos, the love of my life, and
and dearest muse, the best so
together. Thank you life, what

I will need your help to ensu
wooden library shelves, but th
as to become dust-catchers. Sa

Hay que estar aéreo—en la cima de lo inesperado—para que, lo que adviene y en su celeridad demuda, mueva la túnica del estremecimiento y reciba la delicada excitación de la fugacidad requerida por lo eterno

One must remain aerial—at the summit of the unexpected—so, what is to come and in its haste is to alter us, move rather the tunic of thrill to receive the delicate enthrallment of the fugacity required by the eternal

Luis Eduardo Gil Salguero
Escritos, 1934-39
Trans. Cecilia Martinez-Gil

Moisten Harmony

your moist fingers play and my page dowses my hands
in the tacit agreement of your music and my words
rendering promptly rare rhythms
of immersed algae, suspended lotus,
fluctuating water lilies,
as rays of moonlight and sunlight
agleam through the humid air,
watering my language,
swallowing your musical score.

spectacle of humid breath,
Thespian chamber of vowels and notes
pronounced in sighs as desires are,
as a mating in the call and response
of quavers and clefs expressed as onomatopoeias
and ad-libs, rendering song.

your music and my poem
birth the song, its origin of moistness,
so we quench in the succulence of being alive,
in levity.

the sultry craft of voiced sounds
is beating its breathing impulse
inhaling
exhaling
thrusting its pulsation of millennia
in the relentless earthlings' mania
of baring the skin to the awe of experience,
leaning in flesh revealed as blooming flower,
so we may be moist in dew
as divine utterances vest us afresh,
transformed in the duet and in its dance
while your fingers strum,
while my pen inscribes,
in moist harmony.

in situ

There are words out there
clinging but ready to jump us
to make us believe we are being sabotaged, deceived,
believed unfair, unloving, unfit.

Sometimes, there isn't even a word
but a broken utterance
a segue of nonsense getting out of a cage,
a cage that wasn't intended for imprisonment even,
a cage that only meant to contain futile irreverence
—i know that the denotation of the word cage brings a great deal of
weight though, it has baggage, a baggage that we'd rather wouldn't
claim—words as prisoners of the ineffable

But look at it this way,
look rather to this other word
a word that brings forth a better world.
Not a riddle uh uh, it ain't. Even though it might seem it so,
just as the simplest kiss was allegorying understanding:
in case one just happens to cross beyond the ego's frontier.

Then, as corollary, one too gets to bridge
and to breathe in human form
without a fucking conundrum.

It'd be like floating above the water, and yet within.

Isolated by red-wax earplugs so nothing but the water and one are
able to merge, in total inner silence, lingering in peace, in total
fluidity.
As though one and the water were one, one the water and the
water one
forgetting not
what's to be alive,
how to stay
alive.

Morpheus' Dream

The aftermath is the afterword written as poem
side-splitting as metaphors of dreams within a dream
a bet to obliterate the curse and the nightmare,
rib-tickling me to write up anger and hurt:
Lethal allusions to my well-being
Vital metonymies for my new writing.

This is a paradox in shades of blues,
shifting paradigm, as I write the dream
to live thru the oxymoron in its bipolarity,
matching its magnetic extremes
of histrionic hyperboles and insentience's night sentinels

I open my eyes to read
hieroglyphics of loneliness as though carved on sand,
sketched as typhoon and tides flowing on worded lands.

Now the water drops drops,
cumbersome tears pushing down.
Gravity says: "please forgive"
Antimatter says: "please forget"
Y todo falls enmeshed as hybrid emotion
like decanting liquids poured down in frenzy
into the amphora of this page.

Of Frogs and Angels

As snowflakes or sparks speckled from flames and icicles.
Undiscernibly,
words become building blocks of our own Tower of Babel.

Words climb to read our hands, tell us of lifelines:
          our landmarks and their landslides.
Words allow us a glimpse into the future
vesting in front of our eyes however veiled,
          the trance of envisioned visions.
How do we come here? Where do we go after?
I just don't want to go in my sleep though.
I'd rather witness the passage...
          Naïve of me! I have no saying on this, or only rubbish.
Perhaps reasons of voices are unpredictably hidden
as books holding the answer to everything.
          But alas!
I babble that we are desires transpired from thought to life
once the first word of love merged as blood,
and thus, we are their afterlife.
          Because even in the haziest uncertainty
we are all alike, from first to last
frogs of the same pond,
or angels convening not on clouds,
all aligned on shelves, under layers of dust.

writing outside the margins

I've survived the deluge
that pulled me over to the edges,
felt the vertigo of verges
I've climbed the hedges
of these pages:
heard and touched and saw the word
smelled it drank it ate it.

Outside the margins of these lips
pondering on the act of writing
I emote with my shamanic tongue

El genio de la creación
nutre y purifica la naturaleza de mi locura
y no me deja escribir
en los márgenes del error.

Translator:
language auto-detect
auto-correct creating neologisms, inadvertently.

The genius of creation
nurtures and purifies the nature of my madness
and it won't allow me to write
on the margins of er

For, as I poetize, I am in nurtured nature,
primally mating,
within the seams of this white sheet.
Spirited and afire love is,
and within these brimful hems only

me escribe duende

bite the bullet

she posts what she is
as her mouth becomes
her life's partner
and leftovers are discarded in the process of assimilation
of the scrolling reader:
to words lacking minerals proteins vitamins
our bodies say adiós!
And nutrient words of illusions stay
in the forevers of digital signatures
devoured as piece of chalk and ink
chewed as bulleted post-it as sticker on the desktop:

- spread over my poem as though palate of a page
- filter taste-buds, watering meaning, connoting
- obliterate madness by licking the creases
of wrinkled papers
- ooze and dribble pint-sized verbs in the rumples
of discarded layers
- chew copiers to medley only into their middling
idioms
- clench the jaw to shred rejection letters
and ctrl delete
- bite postscripts promising to make them tenants
in the tepid mouth even when they have been
swallowed whole

and yet,
this is forgettable constancy
biting the ███████ dust
of fallen memories████████
and dodging the quick bullets of oblivion
in spite of the instant of digital signs
that in their soundless remarks███████
spit on dead languages which, █████████████ refuse to die.

I lay bare

She opens my book and I see her wetting her index
with the tip of the page
while I lay bare, witnessing my own desire of her gaze
as she turns the page

and the pen ejaculates its toner

so ink as words
become
writers' voices
ground
still in motion
doing
mirages
in-the-making
of benign madness
chronic and indelibly
as topography of calligraphy
on the skin

and we all write with

Transtrommer's Transmutations

There is no cure
for bodies that set themselves on fire.

She is sorceress
gliding through thresholds of memories
uneven and forgiven.

1000 words
etching as surf
upon desired jawline.

He holds the anticipation of crystallized moans
transmuting into heaving cocoons.

man and woman
As dreamed species
alternating themselves in the nowhere of ages.

They remain
gathering in their own mouths
their passion as remnants tasting words unspoken.
Their skins sheltered within their masks
the residuals eavesdropped into realities.

They're still dwelling, in the darkest
sky falling of light
alternating melancholy in the scaffolds
even after the reminiscent shadows of their glow
had disappeared.

And the Letter Goes with the Sayings

Dear John:

Even though birds of a feather flock together, it seems to me—better late than never—that I must come to understand that all that glitters ain't gold. I must write however, as a cat without gloves, because I really believe that all roads lead to Rome. I am aware that you haven't written as much as I have, but a barking dog never bites.

Just the simplest word of all, would have been more than enough, for a word is enough to the wise, and I know, oh! I know that I am wise albeit my confusion when I believed that we were blood...for blood is thicker than water.

Truth may be warm or cruel sometimes, but absences make the heart grow fonder. We've followed the principle that a stitch in times saves nine; yet, it seems that you are the dog that has bitten the hand that has fed it. It goes without saying, with my original way of writing you a letter, that half a loaf is better than none. Surely, it looks as though we are in for a penny, out for a pound, despite that it was clear that there was not to be gained if there was not to be pained.

Thus, I don't regret that I have ventured for I have gained, that I have not cried before I have gotten hurt, and that I have learned to see that all cats are grey in the dark. And because I try to do what's right come what may, every law has its loophole and now we find ourselves learning when it is already too late.

If what was once ours is bygone, I suppose that it's because you believe that sailing smooth seas do makes a skillful sailor. But I will not meet you halfway this time around, as I suppose, you'd have expected me to. Know that I respect that you don't want me to question the mouth of a gifted-horse.

So let's call a spade, a spade, and accept that you would prefer not to scratch my back, even when I am still willing to scratch yours. I see that you'd chosen to bury your head in the sand while I took a chance and burned my candles at both ends.

Nevertheless, I thought twice before I have spoken, and said it all to myself first, but in the end these sayings will speak louder than many words shaped like stones, which I throw without hiding my right hand, which with I write all that has been said and done.

Yours truly, in some ways

Jane

Ps. The postman sometimes rings twice

Thru Writing, Writing Truth

And the mid of night came about and
words were old and faithful
but they were fresh too
and there was no drain
taking them to the ocean.
They were being
inked in here
where the mirror stands me
still
reflecting my transformation without fraud:
and I see now that I am
transgenre

Residuals of Seduction

Let us imagine another
Love poem
Yet
Adding to the canon
To the forces of history
Binding us all in love and in departures
Let's just imagine
A new riddle of hopes
In this emotion that carries us
Through life, going somewhere either way, inevitably.
Let's just imagine that this is
No cliché or archetype
But rather letters
Forming thoughts
All a day longing formulas or metaphors
Weaving me in the synecdoche
Of Nocturnal dreams revealing epiphanies, lucidity.
I am leaning on words as body of these dreams
Inventing a diacritical mark
For my soul, an erasable hyphen between it and reality.
I keep waiting for the breath after the yawn
Weaving and unweaving the roll of the tongue
Looking in the realms beyond the mirror
Drinking the magic potion of sorcery and vision
Writing my love away
Swallowing these letters
Poisoned or nurtured by this ink, at once, as I move beyond
Still living in Imaginaries
I can't digress
Except to it
Over and over
Pulled by forces of energy and matter
The essence and existence of
Us as it becomes I in coalescenscential odyssey.
I am your signifier
You are my signified
I wonder if we should fondle each other
As matter and antimatter in fiery friction
Generating our own Big Bang

What Stays

I have trained myself to hide my pain, so now these majestic sobs come truly as a surprise. My pain is raw. It is primal. Lasher of lucid lucubration of hidden streams and thoughts set asunder or wheresoever they'd rather be. They are however, underdogs barking in underworlds bursting inside brains while pages and neurons befit as words. Sometimes I hear them talking to me, whispering their raspy voices as I read them on their books. I write their willowed words whenever wilted lines of bewildered woe wipe away the shafts of darkness within this bright room. Whatever words come like water and breeze into this affective desert, yet I fail to be satiated. I am this, whenever my lost body finds itself, so I may be oasis, or just one inhabitant coming to life. Thus I read her or him, of her, of him, of me, or whomsoever yearns to emphasize melancholy whereby old desires feed in. Nostalgia is spoken to be retrieved as pages on each story, each poem. It is the departed in here, returning, where authors and readers, are holy mine, as verses sprout from them, while roots and seeds is me from germinal word fields.

Surviving Scales
for Osvaldo Fattoruso

Sometimes death takes it all
but it leaves a will to live
in the gasped awe of surprising insights

I have ink for a while
I have a voice that does not know how to be silenced
I have eyes that do not know how to be muted in tears

And I have a want to write
to live, to inhale and exhale immortally
to touch everything in ecstasy

Sometimes, life surges us all with a single word
shattering us with resisted ease
plunging us enmeshed in Tsunami waves
then, the waves thrash us aground,
and as fish on the dock
we must learn to breathe lashed air in huffs

And you and me and them and we
all come to save each other in our inkling
the hunch that throws us back into the water
to live renewed to breathe abreast again
to write with blooded ink and remain,
forever more in the bequeathed legacies

Hiatus

Overcome the mode
Change the form and shape of the step
Find a trace while walking on new harmonies
Craft the footprint living beyond the instant
Of foot and surface in fleeting contact
Even though I float
Not lost neither aimless
In the fathomed morning of today
Which has already passed
Away.

Cryptic Blues

Species swarming under the rock of tangibility
cast away, they suddenly transcend this darkness
bursting into new life,
then, DNA is liquid, genealogical identity
threatening the demise of ancestry.

Lingering I was— as though I'd have been in flashback mode
foreshadowing this lone reminiscence—
on a ship adrift, lost in its unknown surprises,
while remnants of withered petals
floated in inconclusive blues of aimless waves and formless foam,
humming undecipherable songs amidst the mist
and its mysterious mermaids.

Later yet,
pictures spoke of lives on board over there...
they laid out their secrets of repeatable hodgepodge
respectable murmurs looping or jumping over board,
and in a whirlpool of centrifugal forces
they disappeared without relief.

However,
we are all at present deferring as red herrings,
inextricably bound to our slippery nature of clay,
once the soft grazing of the rain had landed us in the ashore slope,
and we are giants on Earth
at the onset of word, blood, and memory.

Hiatus

All things have been
given to us for a purpose, and
an artist must feel this more intensely.
All that happens to us,
including our humiliations,
our misfortunes,
our embarrassments, all is given
to us as raw material,
as clay, so that
we may shape our
art.

Jorge Luis Borges

Overcome the mode
Change the form and shape of the step
Find a trace while walking on new harmonies
Craft the footprint living beyond the instant
Of foot and surface in fleeting contact
Even though I float
Not lost neither aimless
In the fathomed morning of today
Which has already passed
Away.

Cryptic Blues

Species swarming under the rock of tangibility
cast away, they suddenly transcend this darkness
bursting into new life,
then, DNA is liquid, genealogical identity
threatening the demise of ancestry.

Lingering I was— as though I'd have been in flashback mode
foreshadowing this lone reminiscence—
on a ship adrift, lost in its unknown surprises,
while remnants of withered petals
floated in inconclusive blues of aimless waves and formless foam,
humming undecipherable songs amidst the mist
and its mysterious mermaids.

Later yet,
pictures spoke of lives on board over there...
they laid out their secrets of repeatable hodgepodge
respectable murmurs looping or jumping over board,
and in a whirlpool of centrifugal forces
they disappeared without relief.

However,
we are all at present deferring as red herrings,
inextricably bound to our slippery nature of clay,
once the soft grazing of the rain had landed us in the ashore slope,
and we are giants on Earth
at the onset of word, blood, and memory.

The Cyber Snatcher

I will have to relinquish many of my rightfully owned tropes:
the inspiration of my alliterations, the invention of my metaphors.
I will have to interrupt the conception of dreamt allegories,
the many words that I copulated with in and out of wedlock
with creation and thus, the poems that I lawfully birthed;
even though they're carrying my genomic encryptions,
my accent charmed in riddles of love,
my tone swiveled as dancing cobra
meandering the inheritances of my honed lust…
All evincing the improbable sacrosanctity of my name
and the profanity of the improvable desires of my being.

I will have to burn the ambers sapling on the trunks of my forests
until their agonizing woods and vines are cinders
obliterating into ashes all those wounded whines of mine,
the heavy sighs, the game of hide & seek in the timberlands
the games that crowned the thrones of my book of poems…
Hence, the hearth in my soul will sustain each branding
purging the far-sighted fires in my resolute new word.

I shall not curse its task as if it was one ocean's depleter,
for it is just a sea lamprey, lurking my Orphic waters.
I shall not pity the plagiarist; I shall not revere its sycophancies
I shall shake off its leeches as if they were flying dandelions,
whereupon I'll cast my spell and my altruistic wish of forgiveness,
aside of my own providence like geysers of my mind,
which nurture in trust the oldness of my voice
and render it as random oddity tuned in my pronunciation.

My gibberish speaks me in tongues unraveling my every thought,
transmuting my whims as they write themselves
from my being as gift bestowed upon my page.
And thus, my page sings my voice with the drawls of my instrument:
abiding my laws of life and even of death, my oath to poetry,
replicating only the codes of my covenant,
my reverent devotion to the arts,
the sowing of courtesy to reap good comradeship.

For Calliope, nymph and muse, is my sentinel;
her mother, Mnemosyne, my vigilante; and because the prophetic
Sibyl nurses my breast from its very nipple.
Therefore, I kneel down the altars of inspiration and foretell:
may its burrowing be a sturdy niche, as to never allow sea lamprey
to sink ever again, not even in its shallow waters of sought imitation.

"From Whence Cometh Evil, Thy Sonnet I Shall Sing"

*I seek light, seeking light, doth light of light beguile, for
I seek neither rhyme nor reason that could be seen in my
mind's eye...Nothing either good or bad, certainly, but
thinking makes it so, alas!
However, I do and I make do with my heart on my
sleeve, I breathe life into a stone and thus, I celebrate
the good riddance of ignorance. After all the readings
and all the writings, I still find time to laugh myself into
stitches...Indeed! I am not a strange bedfellow
to literature and there will be more writing and more
reading tomorrow, and tomorrow, and tomorrow.*

Leaning on a Shadow of Grey Hues

i am leaning on a shadow
a shadow of silvery substance.
It recovers my image
in the comic strip instagrammed,
"It was a mistake," It says,
and gestures to log me in&out.

then, It comes
following my every move,
casting my silhouette with a hoary halo.
It is feasible,
It is possible...
the rhapsody of It's nowhereness
i have touched.

i
think that i cannot tether,
that i cannot reach out,
but i do connect and synch It,
to bring It food and water
essentially on&off
to render It as recondite anagram,
and to promise chiseling the shape and form
of It's spot-on shadow and improbable light
into a somewhere entity of sorts.

It is reading now the reluctant poem
that It has drained as i invented It.
You selected It, highlighted It with yellows,
applied track changes, tracked chances,
while i cut and pasted your sentence in It,
as though It was yours
but It has always been mine.

this poem switches code and speaks as ® amidst
a vernacular night, against It's owned shadows.
It is spreading darkness of any today @ sunset
one block North of Sunset Boulevard in the corner
of a Stop sign whence i've read on the speakeasy
"Lo and behold my ©"

magic silver resolution brings shadows
before twilight
over here, on the plains of the mouse pad.
It's gestures are reinvented in bright quality,
Its opacity shines as its reflection renders your recovery,
and i absorb the light, which renders my discovery of It.

It is my poem breakink into prisms of light however,
filtering through It's flat shadow
filling you with holes of light, un-dulling you
through usb hubs.
thus, the unwritten of It will remain compressed
in unfulfillable desires filling folders with leftovers of It,
on each essay, each poem that has ever shed
a printed design on a white page,
confined in a flash drive, passcoded
behind the blinds of It's bunker.

or rather,
this poem should have th-effects of ink
fixing you too, in shadowed and underlined font,
in the hard driven ideograms of font collections
fixing up the poem as host, It's bold type, Its Century Gothic,
as oxymoron of It's simulated existence.
subdued in the genetics of my manuscripts
sour subterfuges are archives of archetypes,
deleble stain where my vision mythologizes
and yet it cannot nonetheless, be archaic.
for then&there, what i failed to remember

a hacker of phantasmagorias hackneyed
as a remote prowler of my erstwhile prophecies
and the metalepsis of my imagination.

i am inept to look into your
(Thoreau's) eyeball,
gaze into your virtual utopias of aloofness,
because i wear reading glasses
which seem to have trapped those involuntary poems
in It's omphalos
and burn them like i would never burn
ancient oracles envisaging my Delphic memories
where you could have been found in remembrances
virtually impeccable, long before It had gone fishing
Its Orphic waters.

Typewriting

A poem is my angel /carrying me ethereally /airlift(ing) (me) benevolently, to the kingdom of this page. /An angel as in "hum yourself a poem" /yielding attributes of my letter A /first to last after Omega had turned /a tribute to transform ME as poem/broken, but only in syllables and morphemes.

Speech act of Angelic letters /universally as language is / filled with the azures of diluted tears, or indelible ink/wanting no Kleenex /no handkerchief but paper to write the Word /band-aiding fragments with wax seal fire-branding the invention/ "Would it suffice?" —I mean—"to cure? To stitch up the wound?" / Palimpsest: re-writing un-lived life could not be just a/patch of liquid paper.

Already this poem is no patch, but a bird/purging me from an underworld. /A poem takes off like blue bird / blue is this flying poem /pushed from the edge of this grief's nest /strategy of resistance to learn to hover/onto cartographies of desires and hopes.

Angel and its L is as goodbye to grief /a waving of the tongue in sure valediction/light as in no more weight /light as in shafts of glow/aligned on a page/it is gravity-binary-of-levity upside down/or rather it'd be glare / golden glare... /Light as in the place I want to be /light as in indigo blue ink that wills me to exist /"which means not following thoughts into its rabbit holes"/"which means no more tears."/ —I paraphrase the Angel—/And thus, Poem Writes Me Whole/ and persistent sadness is no more.

Inside the inkwell

Nobody
questions
flatness
bridges
originswithin
inception

–

Fraught, as one was,
or
shaped, as one is,
one is in the end,
liquid gelling on sheets

–

Everyone
imagines
windows
disclosing
desire
that yields this page
when it's read in
empathy

–

Sometimes
ethereal
screens
butter
fly

Sometimes
formed
like a letter
smitten in consonants
as though the cradle hushed-hushed a word
thirstily, to be breastfed off of random notes
plosive
fricatives
nasal
birthing lullabies
wrought
first in words learning to soothe
and calm

—

against arrogance and anger and angst
there is fortress standing as fence of A's.

then, words are wounds that I lick
for I don't happen to exist in war without a tower
I am not frazzled life, nor a zealous moat declined

—

just writ word of mouth crafting piece of peace remedies as spells of ink
as drawbridge towards imagination. for writing madness is dreaming into
bonfires to be consumed, in comatose.
even when the pencil flat lines me
until I again speak in and out or just

Breathe

A Fix of Ink

I know this poem sounds like a dream
because it comes from a delusion
that I jotted down as notes,
written in the chiaroscuro of one insomniac night,
drawn on the caverns of the self,
in the hollows where leftovers from memories
nest and crack.
These are fragments
upon which I've stepped as I was sleepwalking
and saw you, standing still, suspended in ether:
a floating ghost on the other side of my interface.
And I stepped into this water,
where ripples swelled towards the grotto's walls.

Ripples are now ebbing about my knee
coaxing me to walk on water.
Ripples are now flowing away
and off they go into the molds of a riverbed,
leaving utterly untamable those lions and horses
outlined on the walls of Chauvet Cave,
leaving traces and heaves
as time tracks, as ground cracks,
as waves break and spasm.

Ripples pressing carbon coal
as ink onto the cavern's walls
where owls and eagles fly around draperies of stalactites, perching
on vertices of stalagmites,
insufficiently sketching the sparks of crystal
but not the gritty opacity of chalk
trickling calcite water and red clay.

Incomprehensible ancestral life
rippling me in reasons
fixing me in ink,
tracing me bold as a chiseled silhouette,
etched by fingertips and nails,
opened as red palm to 3D my story:
bleeding my mark
healing on my mark
solidifying the sign,
as I reap me in penned might.

For I am dyed in an ink
that doesn't let me die.

Catharsis

Deer Hunter of young Robert De Niro playing Russian roulette, melting the bare body after the camera panes into the naked torso of Julian Lennon now or young John in my own discovery of his naked body on the cover of *Two Virgins*, when I'd fix my eyes on his censored sex and I'd gulp saliva in curiosity and haste (but not yet then in full blown desire) in the hopes that my grandmother wouldn't notice. I still so wanted him even in the purity of teenager's dream He died when I was sixteen and I wept holding a candle (a lighter actually) in a crowded concert-soccer-field in Montevideo while *Sui Generis* made us sing *Imagine*. Am sorry Dear Yoko, I never felt a figment of disdain towards you just the wonder of you having him nursing love every morning every night songwriting.

Real love comes incomprehensibly for many (for me) but I did dig you Yoko Ono even beyond Starting Over's record, before I was turning around my life south-to-north not upside down not as a merry-go-round not round around like John Keats stirred *Bright Stars* not down and deeper as Werner Herzog's *Caves of Forgotten Dreams* although the letters of the former are on my page and the accent of the latter interlopes my tongue and teeth and mouth...as I articulate *The Beatles'* songs in gibberish while narrating a few inked vignettes Wallace Stevens' style in *13 Ways of Looking at a Blackbird* recited with Hans Zimmer's score.

For I ink from my own celluloid of lights and shadows brittle in air but spirited in echoes I too impress the word as equally plunged in nocturnes inventions like in Chauvet's cave illuminating against the holds and grasps of relinquished but requited memories. Biting the bullet that leaks this ink on my tongue coaxing you to taste me even when you deny me the kiss left on the ~~cave's walls~~ grottoes of Altamira.

I know that this dream comes from delusions that I jot down as notes written in the insomniac night the REM of *vigilia*...drawn in the caverns of the self the hollows where leftovers of memories nest and crack mixed with *fragmentos* of *figmentos* of everything lived through and walked through, stepped upon as I am sleepwalking and saw John standing still suspended in ether, a floating ghost on the other side of my interface, through the screen window of my garden.

Saw De Niro too tapping on my shoulders as he did @ Shutters on the Beach: Hi Mr. Collins! And saw OnoLennon as one, thawing into Keats's burial mask that ~~I had seen~~ I saw at the library's reference desk, scripting odes as if written as on unquenched cellulose films in the inkwells of insatiable vinyl, or on library stacks, and on the verisimilitude of tattooed hides plucked from the tinted root of Stevens' black-feathered birds as all these books on my night table, familiar binds of published press, so I ~~can~~ still guess their presence while they second my dream of books catalogued in library systems of PQ.

For such dream has been writ on water just like Keats' gravestone's epitaph a dream like a blueprint a ~~or~~ watermark of a sublime creature wearing specs swimming the splashes of blood in blue fluid and black graphite. Although in the real nightmare red plasma hit the fan. And thus, I reach out and turn on the light.

Waning gibbous language

lend me a charming muse to rescue me
a voice showing me to craft a few words
to write waning gibbous' affections
so I may not indulge in my defeat

let me borrow a vowel
that knows how to signify my choice
even as I read persuasive trials without articles
so I may act the speech

loan me whetted vibrations, kind voices
so I may not bite a slice of seashore
and grant impunity to ludicrous tribulations

love is defying the split of continents
trespassing lands interloping images of satellite
virtual as love and affairs inheriting augmented visions
zooming into words as seeds randomly disseminated
postcolonially

and if this was going to bid for forgetfulness
i will fail not to record the idle thoughts that
have been forever formulated in the aftermaths
of forecasted e-quakes of Richter e-mails
vanishing as syllables of un-spoken languages
refusing me to be dead, and remaining me
unreservedly unconquered.

Day 22: Waxing Crescent

hesitatant ropes are these lines on my notebook
placing cursor on gps, creating the grid,
yet ceasing to be harmonious, suddenly,
in trodden compositions of lunar cycles…
as we find directions of thumbs-up, or floating icons,
guiding us as computarized recordings voicing gods.

freeways become props, apocryphal set of nowadays
to stage stupid people who cannot use ropes
succesfully, to wrestle gravity with victory instead,
while tears roll-down the windshield, straining clarity,
binding the compassionate chords streaming radio talk,
penciling them as *lágrimas* in the place of words, so
one'd find castaway lines, as if risen by waived shores.

people around us winding in the twilight
leaving patchworks of other people's fingerprints,
sticked in powder to mark accurate traces
identity as bumper stickers which rather shout out
and live no more enveloped in marine fog and smog.

people walking as in daze, as if drifting,
meandering around their own aim…
but managing, nevertheless, to appear after a fixed direction
pinning their autopistas without speed;
only to look at the rectangle of light
that reflects others' inside our hands …their palms.
while we're driving inside the box, the text, the stranged voice
voicing us less and less, utterly;
and yet, the box flashes the poem in the face:
utopian entrance confirmed after tolling
or toiling like moonwalkers in despair to write the sight,
and all around what we see as flaneurs of the cityscape,
as city slickers dwelling in urban slams.

* * *

Escape, otherwise, to tackle the questions from your eyes' enigma,
to ache the ax falling on the tongue
that would answer the shining ray on the mouth
and ban the books, as guillotine of free speech.

I hear the sound of your expected
Call and Response, our taking two to tango,
and I mouth you and word you dialectically,
in the prescient kiss under the clichéd moonlight
to write my own dreamt novel of an existent unrealm.

You have the tips of my fingers
ready to tap the screen and sculpt you as avatar,
text you sex you write you up as if real,
yielding catharsis to your voice as if soundfull,
dwelling in crescent junctions of unmated thoughts
and virtual divides spoken in Esperanto.

My sensitive fingertips score points:
you'd say right now what path I should walk,
you video-game me and say how you'd feel if
I sms you in everlasting love, despite the clicking sounds
announcing the glitched loop, as intermitent ellipsis.
because this game is never over.

* * *

Quills of a rare bird

Make you believe you can learn to speak
a rare language. Made me believe in your letter...
But you wonder:
Can the right words be jotted down on your page?
What is the right message today?
Would I say too much?
Could I mislead her?

This bird's feathers can fly above
and rise beyond your walls
fly the immensity of the blue ether
with its tangible wings flapping air like book' lappets
tracing in the air utterances
like perfect brushstroke sketching an airborn poem
ascending towards the horizon
circunvolating the curve of Earth
as we read from afar,
To Whom It May Concern

But what is it what I should say?
The simplest words, the most profound?
Or it would be just too soon
or too much
too risky to open up?
Hence, he would think I am a stalker of English language

SMS to BFF:
i just want to speak about
el o vi e Seriously
without el o el
hoping that he doesn't go
like double-u tee ef

It can always be blamed
on the darn autocorrect though

Diacritics and circumflexes,
cedillas and umlauts,
to fully stop as emoticons of impressions and effects
smiley faces, colon (:) winking and P's tongue-out-cheek
hover-boarding on high tides of expressions
saying it all in signs signifying known gestures
emotional IQ of immeasurable gauge
while a rare bird overflies granting a plume to draw a paper trail,
to type of desires and of love @ first sight
while meaning is already long gone
and its creator an inkless chi sitting Shiva

Vi®gil in Dazetown

For I have ideas nesting in my dermis
intuition of the flesh penned in coherence
there and here
below my navel,
and when poems stammer the embrace
the word of a mouth uninvites a kiss
that once and again was precluded

There is your finger
telling me that you are
steering the sunrise
as if the sun were a shell breaking to life
from the insides of
a cocoon of extinguished fires within
enabled to emit night-rays to burst it all out
in safeguarding ways;
but the sun is not as you have written it up

I have so much to say, so many poems to textualize
these hibernated contexts,
but alas!
I remain still
immobile my muscles
cautious my organs
after you had muzzled me and blocked me
as writer, rendered me invisible as woman

There, behind my eyelids
sheltered in the shades are the shadows of my eyes
suddenly carrying away the images
that you've contained and I now release
as new-fangled poems

But I see you cantering ungreened fields,
cursed in the outlined night-rays
of borrowed moons and stolen affections.
And here are my release notes,
you should click "Agree to the terms"
but read them first notwithstanding my fine-print.

My eyes let go of you, tributary of tears,
and pain runs away from me
through underground drains, down the Pacific
so my former tears disappear in the coldest mouth,
or in a bigger sea of Atlantic sour salt
and not in your cesspit

Out of your ill dream
I rise as vigilant walker
un-dazing this lurid nightmare for good.
In the serenity of my wakeful streams,
I scrolled down this page to its end
and find your footprints fading
off of your empty cartridges.

Capturing fall-nesses

Instant falls into loving lake
With sounds falling
In this fumbling autumn of innocence
Fuscia is the instant that falls
Playing ukulele as fountain of sounds
Which fall too
Into my feeble eye
Falcon flying
Never falling
Trailing a scarf of wind floating in flight
Following the afterwards of its winding airlift
Like oak leaves leave trees to fall onto my desk
And onto my desk I fall
Fall into this frazzled instant of
Fall as autumn's waterfall
At rainy and fragile noon
A noon falling upon the sea
The instant figmented by the eye
Capturing fall-nesses
And never failing to write in the fall
Of falling out of love

Graffiti Sacrifice

Feather lingering
Stripping its bird
plucked by
obtuse wind
as obsolete presage
of long-ago-shared-ink
as smoke seething the distance
between the wall and I
risking light
to shadows of night vision

Dreams wrote convictions
convictions followed retaliations
marked with symbols made of
back slash/forward slash
and dot com
turning themselves into doorknobs
flashing intermittent red lights
as caution to trespass
trigger warning if entering
asterisk rotating as black flash
star shaped white
blue snowflake
flickering via yellow limelight
weather's sun
radioactive
stop sign (stained of spray paint)
anus, Uranus, ass
nether hole for jerking jerks
into Dantesque's realms

Spray paint lingering breath
before hitting the wall
doing illegal fucking when
blinding anarchy
has broken streetlights
into sporadic scratches on the bricks
a hiss running the space
shouted slang redeeming the space
voiced speech act on a fence

Who cares?—etches the Scribner
and it is never a question
nor a paste-up stenciled sticker
nor a rejected invitation
just a tag against a banned buff
and all is words of rebellion
against these lies

From king to knight to page
back to back and back to the beginning
back to the un-future of dark cities
where
a bribe is tantamount to the spirit of salvation
Ephemeral as time
Staggering
Daggering
Malingering
as patch on the city's hedge
but never a mural

Distance between wall and mirror
tested in soreness
oil means water-repellence
leaving the painter thirsty and the graffiti indelible
in dispersion
as un-togetherness
or stammering loving
like trains bygone
while neglected pennies and tokens remain
muggy and soiled
along the station's platform

paled as nocturnal shadows
homeless bodies walking under unnamable bridges
burnt bridges
untagged corners
ruins as frontiers of the past
or speech acts performed on planks
where once upon a time
we sacrificed our bodies
and no one cried out

(a)void

He
who walks my city
as though surfing Atlantic waves.
And him
staying in farewells as if he had never
gone gone.
He
who touched me in waking memory to feel today.
And him certainly
kissing every inch of my skin
as if his lips would had the time.
And him
with his
candy tongue
with his hands finding me away
with his eyes knowing me blindly
him whom I can taste even then, but never now.

Although it's him
in every minute of my sleeping past
taking my mind to where only he belongs
and dragging my body where I dreamt it to dwell
while sleepwalking the Hpnotiq blankets of a spell.

Hence, I tatoo the virgin continent, south to north
and songwrite.

Tattoo

The answer to this mess
comes in the inner voice and its finger
pointing to an inexact piece belonging everywhere.

Loneliness has taken a humane form
and when she cries
her tears land inside my ear
unreservedly deafening me.

I could hammer the results, clinch with the wrench,
screw-drive the postulations
as I spread the pieces of the clock over my bed
inventing the unity of time once again.

I want you not to write the truth just yet,
doubling the no: the do not, the I dunno, equal to positive,
don't want you to know nothing just now
whilst time is a SalvadorDalian trope and it ain't graspable.

The answer is time and space: chronotopia where I,
stand across the railroad shaped as sonnet
wait for the siren to stir my ear with its spoon lever,
and scoop the smithereens of me as iambic syllables
as I'd have played hopscotch jumping the pentametered rails,
beseeching the sun to reach my feet centering me
while it shines its yellow rays over my rotating soles.

What time is it? It is ABAB CDCD EFEF GG
Resolving the melody in its root chord,
via harmonic progressions.
Damn it! I should just take this train...

Women of Newfangleness

women

who run with wolves / gale of forces howling laughter to the 100%
full moon of tonight / and there / in here / there is / a silver coat
illuminating paragraphs without full stop / unraveling words beyond
the heath / splashing us out as silhouettes of mud and clay / squirting
blazes spat by the hearth / where nothingness agonizes against the
brightening newfangleness of existence / ... For—as always— /we live
more / in gender fluidity. / Or else, / Earth: open up and swallow us
whole.

Trojan Horse

Deception is a pen but not like mine tsk tsk
Deception is false deities lurking my heart
Feeding as leeches off of the streaming of my blood.

Deception writes with fine point though,
Sharpie sharp words indelible but unphonetic
as ink unwashed of digital signature on social network:
CHARACTERS encrypting shape-shifting deceits,
as though on stone tablet, engraved and crafted
but only carved by the impostors' chisel.

I was doomed in my own indigo dye
after my ill-fated foreword was under surveillance.
But I have prologued my return of Phoenix,
soaring the skies of hyper-reality
flying above meadows of immortal words,
hovering over ars poetica and defences of poetry
while the intruders burn their essence of papier-mâché
in sky high pyres of terrible flames
and my status updates key their eulogies
as Wildean epigrams.

I inhabit a city without end.
The unreadable symbols of creatures
were written however, as if they edged
against virtual abysses of loneliness.
They grumbled in cacophonies and saturated sounds
chiming notifications of chain-emails, as stalkers, finding
reverberation via junk mail and blocked spam.
They targeted my accent and pronunciation
but failed to solve the riddles of my own charms.

One true-self, imprinting the boundaries
where I was pushed back, spellbound,
to my table of contents, to my glossary.
I am now recovering all my drafted chapters
in Roman numerals; I am rebooting in forewords
as my ink-stained index finger reaches the button
and presses on the icon shaping power
allowing me the view into a room of my own
through this window from where I see
my sea of words, these blank pages that are no more.

My Page recovered: I am ready to re read it.
A Page retrieved: I am ready to save-it-as
MINE.

In the silence of the night,
in the inaudible algorithms of mathematical lattices
my pen still writes on paper keeping me safe and sound
(on the acknowledgements' page).

Life goes on after the endnotes,
and I am warmly tucked in book's jackets,
even after burning all the letters (from a to z),
in the epilogue of formatted hard drives
in the afterword of extemporal time machines
on the bookmark of anachronistic time tunnels.

I write this epitaph before Troy burns the galleys,
the fire pits of infringed memories are now ashes
dwelling in the dwellings of Hades, its conflagrations:
as I walk on the perpetual embers
of epic revivals of my storytelling.

Abecedarian

Azimuth's axis above Amber air
after Achilles ached away anxieties
amidst Aurora borealis breeding, birthing breath
borrowing brightness, bursting barred blackholes
beaming balms, banishing Castor's cataclysm.
Cataloguing: causation/causality-cyclic cosmology.
Constellations
clustering chaos, cajoling COALS,
doppelganger's dream deciphers DIAMONDS.
Dream devours darkness, despair...
demigods' deeds defy decibels,
elapsing ellipsis, ensuing ethereal embers
eluding eclipses, extinctions
etching egalitarian **Earth**. Except
fugitive Fahrenheit fluctuating from feigning fables
fumbling façades, frosting furnished figments.
Form, generating growing galaxies,
gleaning glistening grains,
garnishing gazed gloss.
Gleaming Gamma glows honor hailed Halo
hiding hiatus.
Human holds humble hearth
harboring heliocentric helix
illuminating iridescent ions,
infrared indigo
invisible inertia invoking interaction-
imminent interstellar intensity.
Joyful jewels jiggling jungle's jaw,
jolting jaspers joining juddered jet,
jointing Joules,
knitting Kelvins,
keywording kinship's knowledge
kites' keepers: Knights; kind Kairos' kissers;
kernels' love +
Luna's Luminescent Laws
(locking ~~Leviathan~~).
Lion's lore lurking libels
leaping latitudes: Leonid Meteors.
Mimicked memory molding mirages,

mirrors mastering modern miracles,
magic made nowhere nebula, near nanoseconds
negating Newton's notion,
Nereid's nether, navigating Nadir's nova.
Or Orion orbiting oracles of Omega,
oscillating ornaments over origin??
Oxymoronic planet!
Panstellar paradox: Perseus plume [pixeling] prototypes,
Prometheus pioneering phosphorus,
Pollux's pulsar quavering quasar.
Quake quelled in quantum quarks;
questing qualms, quashed quartz, quenched radar,
rotating radiantly,
reciprocating redshift reflection,
refractioning requited resonances:
romance resolving rings. Saturn substantiating
solar solace, shivering shells
shedding stellar scintillation
sidereal shadows = spectrums.
Tangential transition this theorem towards telepathy
tailoring the telling, tailing
through tailgating upwards—
ultraviolet upper universality.
Ultimately, unwinding umbilical urge under unlovable
un-uniformed urban voyager of vortexes.
Visionary veiling vibration, velocity's verbs
voiding vacuum, vexing vermin.
Warped world,
wavelength weaving wavering words
with whispered wishes willing weakened weapons
war xenophobia x-terminated. X-rays x-citing x-clamations.
xilophonic x-tasis, x-suberant x-cilaration,
x-suding x-samples x-traordinaire yonder.
Yarns of yearning years yelped, yanking yards,
yielding youth [yin&yang] yawning yoga, zooming,
Zen, zigzagging zone, zipped zombies,
zag zodiac zesty zeal: Zahir's Zenith.

Mentorship

I know that profé'd almost do anything for me,
such as hold my pen, clear my lenses,
assign papers and e'en grade them,
coax me to critique
art and literature,
as profé' mentors
me…

Now, I am wondering amidst these lectures
What'd be writ on the exempted list?
Wouldn't a kiss enact'em teachings
more than a speech?
Respectfully, Profé
instruct the art
of a kiss.

Students and Professors

Have you forgotten the pains of knowledge?
You are there: I can see your eyes gazing
behind the crystal of your ivory tower
looking down
looking down at me

I am
still standing on the greener grass of surprises
still devouring beauty in every page I read
marveled in words, in the marbles of sentiment.
I look up to the page foreign or anew
words built like sand castles, house of cards,
words carved on gravestones, inked or graffitied
words on palimpsests, on papyrus
words with images that can be tasted
voices that can be touched
riddles that want to be thread-bared
symbols coding decoys
cyphers enacting exactness of time
riddles as hieroglyphics of dyslexia
palindromes of semic writing
in the inner semantics of the self
and on the pages that I print
on the walls I graph and script
the relics that I synch to update me
the ruins that I fix in ink

The human condition
mutates and evolves from the same
DNA of signs
and I have them, write them, read them
I own them, I am aware of them
I want to know of them
in the now of what they signify
of my existence
my free will
my choice of chance
my providential charms
my fixing me in poetry
handright writing it

I, on the other hand
could not forget the pleasure of knowledge
because I am here
on the grass
laying to gaze up to the sky as a page-turner.

I am not like you, ghouls hiding behind the glass window.
I see you and you aren't like me
Crouching to birth meaning
Standing to tremble in beauty
Bending down to sweat these words
Bending backwards and under new lenses
Heaving utterances generated in the lungs
Speech acts of pain and pleasure
Reading poetry
Words as lyrics
Singing them (actually)
Trying to sing them to my own beat
Trying to sing them as I imagine the song playing
Sung by original worders:
Bards and luthiers of literature, lovers of stories
Fictionists of experience
Weepers of emotion
Criers of reason

I have no master's degree
I ain't no master
I am a blue-collar poet
I am a wordsmith
I am worder
I am
Word and Invention

Whereas,
You have forgotten that these sheets bear life,
History of empathy.

And that you could witness it
Not in the field
Not in the work
But in the fieldwork.

You see them as if they were dead carcasses
You examine them from behind the glass
You done seen them beauties
You ain't gonna touch them pages
You are blind to see the way I am in them

I thought that I wanted to be there too
next to you
but me ain't want to be the One no mo' but the Other

I'd rather stay on the grass
I'd rather keep trembling
I'd rather sing and tell and write
I'd rather poetize and
Speak the word to make new worlds

I choose to be a blue-collar worder
even if that means that I might be re-building
Your Ivory Tower

The Purloined Papers

Ghostwriter scripts the lost solemnities
secluding the Writer's mind,
makes do of the Reader not of the Author.

And the Writer dries then its ink
in sourness and solitude.

The Ghostwriter
utters cacophonic assonances
un-rhyming the Writer's kernel
disputing,
shrinking,
sullying the story.

Imitation not intimations,
so intimacy between word and legend is
Forever Lost.

The Ghostwriter besieges through College-ruled paper,
scribbling with erasable pencil, with a fissured quill,
trying to warp time,
emptying the virtue of the tale
onto a purloined manuscript,
filtering folio bound in threads,
blurring tones and tonalities, erasing illuminations
bold type of expressions of many greys,
wordless utterances: fallacies and sophisms
re-written by the ink of the Ghostwriter
defying memory, authenticity,
effacing the Writer's ink-stained fingers,
the Writer's experience
and even effing Johannes Guttenberg.

For such quill of Ghostwriters cuts jaggedly,
as it designs a Rough-Draft,
still coaxing the ink to run deeply and afar.

Ultimately, the ink runs down
towards the epicenter of its truth:
the genuine gens, the magna magma
the living pulse in the Writer's wound
the speaking act of the Writer's word,
the Writer's testimony.

A page shrills on its edges
gliding in ruled tourniquets
paper cuts as sharply as a blade
but the bleeding is of muted utterances
on the Writer's testament.

And if it does,
it is the Writer who bleeds its penmanship
on the transliterated tales written on purloined papers
by one alleged Ghostwriter, getting paid.

Azar

Gauging nothingness that fills my years,
embracing less love of solitary awakenings.
I am torn in despair,
thorn in anger, thrown in parchedness,
and I spy my own deceiving eye,
starved of illusions, numb in dormant dreams.

It is you who I am then inventing
in my restless poetry making, so
I float in the oasis of scripted dreams,
I enter the dark poem,
I contemplate within, within the silent poem.
Only in here you come to live,
to craft me, to make me,
to make out me, to do me
in the randomness of chance: azar.

But out there I am a seagull lost
adrift in reality,
filling lines between lines
with the vacuity, the sadness, the blankness,
all the scarcities of your illusory presence.

Come. Come to embed me bodily again,
craft me as poem, for I am so lonely on this block!
Come to silver-tongue my ripe brims
of wakeful and incandescent mornings,
when you'd be nevertheless, not allowed
to borrow more than just a handful of my dreams.
So I may only awaken certain illusions
weighted under the gravity of your pound key.

Indigo Blur

Then I see your tongue
slithering magic over me
a melody of sound transforming me
in the in word
in *yo digo* indigo is within
so i dig in and find my voice.

My words are written ink
bled in blues
traveling the miles
of unpredicted canvases and music sheets.

I can see my desire as a helix
twirling indigo blur centered in axis
bold as love intoned by Jimmy Hendrix
fearfully audacious guitar riffs
in the coincidental emanations of blues soundtracks.

You are spacing into Hokusai's wave
as ekphrasis of desire, of palettes and paint brush
an idea blurred within water-colored nuances.
I read your creed tinted on parchment
touch its pigment of sky's illumination
see how the brush conceals forecasting clouds.

I sniff your body as if we were lions of the steppes.
Lions starving and lurking their preys
behind meadows of narcissus,
panting in the trepidation of anticipation,
as we prescient the emerging danger
from unwavering, altering seas.
This midnight silence rolls down the incline as poems
translators of unseen moonlighting
and I harbor truth in the shelters of my mind
in the open palms of my hands.

I see beyond the gestures of your fingers
serving ink inside my cupped hands
when I sink in dreamed paragraphs
inking brush-strokes of indigo blurred
and anchored in the perpetual tides
of round and round record of a phonograph.

Workshopping: indigo

Then I see your tongue.

You speak the words that
I expect to hear.

My words are written ink,
bled in BBKing blues
traveling miles
of unexpected voices
concealed in memory.

Desire is a helix
twirling in the axis (Jimmy Hendrix' Bold as Love)
and a wave unfold with one such background music

You are facing a Hokusai wave.
Material notion: creed written on parchment
with sky illumination
veiling its own veil with clouds—
a contract to rise me, storm me.

I sniff, and your body
starves and lurks forth, almost motionless
behind meadows of narcissus,
in the valley that a Goliath wave will fill.
I am undone in this ocean unweaving us
immerse in the scents of intangible millenia.

Universe of words,
feed me, so I may come to you
without thinning frontiers of light.

It is midnight silence falling
under your carnival mask, moon lightening.

Come and kiss me on the mouth
taste us meeting limelight tongues,
investing nights in beehive moods.
in the nightly dusts dripping glow...
Come and kiss me.

I see, beyond this indigo ink,
gestures of your fingers brush stroking me.
I feel as vinyl, circling in tiny deaths that reach me
as though after dancing a tune sung by Nina Simone.
when I sink in you, in knots of shudders
making me up, immortal in paragraphs and canvases
embedding me in new awakenings
of indigo blur
as the bells toll the midnight hour
on a second night of one full moon shedding twilight
over the mountain inclines and their valleys.

Because the lion has left me extended
and unsheltered from the teeth
of a clawing blue dot; a full stop
as the indigo ocean has ebbed once more.

Editor's voice over and et all (the assumptions):
who press Del key, command,
select and drag out
then empty the trash can,
[which banishes paper with crinkling sounds]

An on the crystal ceiling
a bubble of water has formed
suspended in trembling indecision
until gravity withholds no more
and it drops, freefalling on this page
cracking it and diluting it all.

Prewriting Exercise: fountain of ink

Fountain of ink
does not ploy deceptions, no.
Pen surges to create illusions,
so play in them, within,
dance at their beat
script your own scenes
enable yourself to animate infinity
in this timed timely second
within the utopian frame of these pages
where poems read your delights and my sins
without tricking the reader not to believe
without misleading the writer not to relive.
As words and writers and readers meet
in the promise and the pledge
the oath supped under our tongues
as poems swallow you
as you feast in your echo of my own patois
Cuming to Live
Coming to Life
Spoken verb
while this story becomes verve that thrives.

Dreamt

Doubts like shadows dreamt in the impossible
Rubbing illusions as ghostly spectrums of indissoluble light
Eavesdropping in the silent the same word
Aspiring to breathe resolute metaphors, alliterations, a chiasmus
Masks of lips and tongues un-muted in mutiny
Towards a certain certainty reversing that, which is yet

Undreamt.

Draft: drink from my ink

My desk
shaped
like
capital l

_

Poetic liquid
dribbling from
Blake's angels perched on my bookshelf
sprinkling golden specks on grimy dust

thoughts as sugar, encoded as unitext
in the ol' DOS
of floppy disks

sagacity of numbers writing code
underscore dash
password fettering key chain
hiding my sins of a Lady Byron
turning me
in cleansed_
clear drop: inked
from lucidity of tear:
blurry screen that still invents that poem
that will remain unseen

I was grounded below underlines
where there was
un mot comme une marque d'encre
a speck of dust,
a mote of greyish graphite
a carbon allotrope
a trope of language
a

.

of ink
over here too .
look it read it!: .

without the writer typing the full stop
with the teacher signifying the punctuation mark
with the author signposting, the publisher striking it…
for the source will follow within quotation marks

it is a "."
not a typo of printing press
uh uh

here…see? .
—select thicker deeper bold
                    take cursor to upper bar to insert,
                    then select symbol, re size
there . see?
font size tells me the importance
of screams built on capitalization
but you see instead the tip of my finger
leaving a word like a wafer in your mouth
_

a letter per capita tasting like sacred wafer
it's the initial or the dot to exclaim, to ask
what?
Or
what!
It is a splash of ink like a hegira of a lingua franca.

Google (as transitive verb) an image of a splash of ink…
many graphic designs found after Boolean query
and or not, Kierkegaard's Either Or—Søren Enten Eller.
Google Images showcase photos (shopped)
[They are all pixeled and pixelated:
No one seems a true scan of true ink]

Am I being deceived?
uh uh…this is Coleridge's suspension of disbelief
it is just another illusion:
the impression that has been invited instead
to make of my tongue a fictional open act

I lift the
veil of illusion
not to reveal its trick, but to trek it in its space!
Thus, this page is not vellum but palimpsest
where calligraphic symbols persist beyond the tint

The purpose is to make you believe
that I haven't typed a word in Word,
that you are casting the felt while reading it
and scribbling the grapheme on skin
with ink charting the pulp
as flesh on a sheet, with a fountain pen
a MontBlanc, ascending Shelley's summit
guided by a calligraphy's chart
of Taccia's penmanship,
finding the fountain of ink gushing from its sharp nib
after the sac had fed the barrel with its blue gen
and the squirt of ink is not other than my sperm
as seed birthing signs and signifiers on sensitive leaf

Most definitely, I ain't here to deceive you
but to make you live forever
feeling my words licking the gradient of your epicenter
spawning—temperature
as Keats' negative capability harbors behind
your retina of woman or man
as your hands grasp and hold my head
by its temples of hermaphrodite
and you read me
like you'd read a book at take off gripping me,
turning the page at landing in yellow airport mode
and wiping your mouth
with your index and middle fingers
as you live up fiction once more
and once you'd conceded a trek

I am self-pleased pleasing you as well
in the plenty heritage in Borges' typewriters

iGoogle typewriters' sounds
downloadable clip promising to type
on iMac/MacBook keyboards—
an MP3 of Royal/Olivetti

I poetize, feel the Words-Worthy of overflows
birthright of evanescence
to shape me obsolescently
of poets of the past now cyber paged

I
feature them as template
so I believe them, so you believe
in my yet-unwritten Kabbalah poem
budding under my reading glasses
as the typewriter clatters sounds
that we all so quaff

and in this telling and writing
demons are effaced
verses are fixed, moods emoted,
bonded as newest truths on trundled papyrus
played dimensionally in your mind in blue ray
streaming noiseless sounds
as if your fingers had rolled the dice
after you've read me
to mend our broken hearts,
to glue our torn pages,
to restore the scratches across the vinyl
to patch the abraded frames of the film
as this poem mouthfuls us

                    drink from my ink

                    and you'll live forever

Suspension of Disbelief

Plot:
One day
This love is going to die
Still/Motionless
Because you are
Certainly
Killing it

Lucubration: I am still asking why
and yet
it looks as if
naturally, you were writing fiction
but
you'd never even written the acknowledgement page

Update fix: the writer just wrote it,
on Google docs as remote, invisible typist
or did its novel's character,
endowed with artificial intelligence.
The narrator is omniscient:
his pining is motionless, still. His flatness kills me though.
Should he be developed further for another tale?

Editorial Suggestions:
Have the guts to cut a full entire paragraph
which equals to…unlimiting the imagination
engendering a proactive readership
find him a lover make him risk falling in love.
There should be a conflict, and its ensuing dénouement,
as an expected thrill, edging the body on the reading.

Chapter X: he forfeits his chance
his dream-coming. His locution appears as anachronic,
unless I fail to forget that you've written fiction.
Final reading does not offer solution: no closure.
You need to write the transformative flight.
You have The Pledge, and you showed The Turn,
but lack
The Prestige

Vampires' Appeal to Dusk

This is a bitter tongue licking this conflict
whiting it out, obliterating your presumptions
of my blood with ink's elixir.
You are quote blocking sourcing my thoughts
with Thick fiber-tip of impermanent marker:
smear-free is this tongue's tip wiping you off
of my trademark from my neck to your sheet.

Amidst the clouds and the blizzard
I sought your embrace
<Count on it> you said
and time came to pass
after you once-upon-a-time-me
and we couldn't live
happily-ever-after because after
never came back.

I felt grains of sand then
inside my eyes, couldn't read what I've written:
couldn't hold on to my mark.
Gaze blurring my skin roughed by your bare sensuality.
And then, this cold moor, clenching your isolation,
confiscated your eyes!
No more sand, but a cave
a dark tunnel towards your daily silence.

You're lurking sensuality,
stalking are your ominous eyes
reading me to inscribe
your existence as I write the page
that you've transcribed.

'twas the only darkness that I liked that day though,
'twas the only silence that comforted me
in the reading me within
for a banned book leaves its characters undead
like vampires who know how to flee daylight
and yet, they don't know how to remain unfed.

So should you have read me at least once,
would have had me, supposedly,
worded up all over again
like in a hypothetical forever before,
streaming my mouth with your fingers
strumming in kisses in feverish bliss
lips plucking the strings of my innocence
singing unwritten words like
bards've sung before, and griots'd tell afterwards.

Eyes still dim as they have been, ever;
they are proof readings of your kismet, or
carbonic copy sheets of my writing.
Immerse in the absolute nostalgia of this river
of sentences, you remain however,
flowing to the past of a never before,
explaining the spoken word of now:
for the script of your play is of today
poured over me, editing my body before dawn
just before you were beginning to tear down,
these paper walls—to attempt to burn me like Troy
before the dusk is ready as one is now,
to be pressed in trays of movable type
whence all the words bleed in black.

Blogger in Bowties

Duende
giant and bold,
living on the planes of paper, within and yonder,
untie me, unravel me as codex.
Today, come to read me like no one has
ever
filled my pen,
feel me as you speak to me
the word *duende*

My walk is sensual on these lines
my swagger carves my path,
the curves of my profile, the identity of this poem,
duende's form and depth, Duende's spell.
We make way, fearless, crossing the brink
toward the core beneath this sheet
into the thickest forest where x means *duende*
where y means *poem*
where the heart of lightness dwells.
I, with Duende on a quest for the Rosetta Stone.

Should I were to find it,
I would be the one sucking every tongue
even yours. Me, tonguefeeding your everyword
I would be a translator of Babel,
a scribe of all the phonemes of the world,
I would be language-fed
wearing *duende* organically,
a second skin however never second-guessed.
I would be able to fall and spring with ink,
and write not of trolls and their stupid bowties
and read not of their malice and derision. Rather,
write of *duende* and in Duende's stead.

Now Duende scripts talking leaves out of tree barks
spelling my words from layers of his heart of geyser
and ink saps over me, like marine lava
sluicing me in xylem
as if *duende* were washing Lilith's forsaken valleys,
un-blackening all of those stained letters,
expelling deception
and other horrors of cons' landfills.
I'd pour milk over myself, legible spelled
recording the page itself, nurturing it
with the decipherable ink of my breast
as I latch this *poem* cradled in warmth
so I may be one audacious, perpetual,
sourced
Poem
In
Duende.

Epilogue

i least of all
had a clue of a verb signified.
at the top of the hopscotch
the doodle of a pining sun
was drawn on me as Henna tattoo
like a dying star of opaque yellows,
now smudged dust on my skin
with faded verbs of desires jumping
square to square
over my body of chalk.
the verb as rock, reaching the mouth,
to mouth-to-mouth
not to give breath, not to hop onto hope,
but to fill not me with solar radiation instead,
to blacken and taint me,
to dry me in crushed sketch,
until I drift in dizzying loops, airless,
afar from the trace, the trend, the thread,
the enlightened trek as Pegasus,
as though I was instead
in merry-go-round riding solo
after a chimera, a sham, a fib
but never after a dream

i most of all
remain stationary but huffing and neighing,
retelling routes of rotation, crafting charts,
spacing in the boxed reminders of anticipated
checkered flags,
nickering to prophecies of trumpet sounds
at the threshold of a starting gate,
but not for a race that i'd refuse to run,
not even to reach the sun at the finishing line,
but to gallop and gallop
in an unsaddled unreined flight

i betwixt it all
circle back to the estimated melting of Icarus' wings
who fell as he was reaching the sun,
or to meet Bellerophon who fell off of Pegasus
as he rode him to meet one mortal woman,
who fell in, and fell out of love and fell too...
and once they had all hit the ground
there is again a spill of ink
dripping off of the jagged tip of quills,
the liquid that washes away the traces of hopscotch,
the greyish doodled concrete,
the squares drawn over my black and white body of ink

i beyond it all
allow the washing to begin:
proofreading names and editing errors
polishing away the stains over my body of poem,
revising it as though skywrit by a humble jockey
riding a winged unicorn,
enabling it to tether the word to a ferris wheel
so this poem may fly after the high hop,
the giant leap,
the Geronimo jump,
the rides turned journey,
the games turned journaling
that you now read to dejavu it all
including,
the hopscotch, the merry-go-round, the ferris wheel.
because names and errors
are now parts of a speech,
allusions to legends and myths,
reversed metaphors of misfortunes,
cautionary tales, and above all,
they are this collection of poems
where names and errors
are all faded below clouds,
whited-out and blanked off,

as crumpled papers
tossed and slam dunked into the trash can app.
while in here, on my last page of "a fix of ink"

i for starters
impressed my expressions
as etched on skygrounds
and took off of the pages,
remembering rewriting retelling reviving
rebirthing, by way of words,
for

i last of all
inscribed them as tales,
instill them in myths,
played them as though children's games,
so this inefaceable body of poem
is
at last
airborne, a word like a kite
taking flight

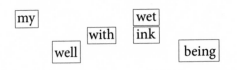

and thus,

we've been

fixed
with
ink

Cecilia Martinez-Gil is the author of *Psaltery and Serpentines*, a Book of Poems, published by Gival Press (October 2010). This book was also a finalist for the 2010 ForeWord Reviews' Book of the Year Award for Poetry, finalist in the USA National Best Books Award for Poetry—2010 and Runner-Up for the 2010 Los Angeles Book Festival Poetry Award. A chapbook version of *Psaltery and Serpentines* was also winner of Finishing Line Press 2010 poetry award.

A graduate of USC with a B.A. in Comparative Literature and Cultural Studies, Cecilia Martínez-Gil has an M.A in Hispanic Languages and Literatures from UCLA and an M.A. in English and Creative Writing from Loyola Marymount University. During her tenure at UCLA she taught Spanish, and at LMU she taught English and Intro to Poetry, as a teacher associate and as teaching fellow respectively. She has taught Spanish and Philosophy, Creative Writing Workshops and Seminars for Middle and High School students. Cecilia is Adjunct Professor of the English Department at Santa Monica College where she teaches English Composition, English Literature and Latin American Literatures in translation.

Her poems have been published in Voices, A Santa Monica Women's College Publication, Anthology of Latin American Writers in Los Angeles, Imaginarias: Antología de Poesía (Ediciones de la Crítica, Montevideo, Uruguay), and in her first chapbook *Muecas de Fósforo* (Ediciones Caballo de Fuego, Montevideo, Uruguay 1987). Her work as a journalist/writer (articles, interviews, reviews and critiques) has been published on several Uruguayan newspapers and magazines (1987-1989).

She also co-wrote and played the lead character in the award-winning (SODRE) experimental Video Arte Poesía *Itinerarios* directed by Roberto Mascaró (CEMA 1988).

Originally from Montevideo, Uruguay, Cecilia traveled extensively for South America, Europe and the Caribbean. She lives in Santa Monica, California with her husband, Federico Ramos, a composer and guitarist, and their daughter Magaluna, an emergent singer/songwriter.